I
Need
To Talk
To You,
God

by MARTHA POPSON

The C. R. Gibson Company
Norwalk, Connecticut 06856

For you, Joy —

WITH TENDER FEELINGS
OF EMPATHY IN YOUR ILLNESS...
AND WITH A HEAVY HEART
BECAUSE OF YOUR SADNESS
AND SORROW IN SICKNESS.

I LOVE YOU —

MAY THIS LITTLE BOOK
PROVIDE A LITTLE CHEER,
A RAY OF HOPE, A SHARE OF
SUNSHINE RIGHT NOW —

To Ray
M.P.

Mom
December, 1984

Copyright © MCMLXXXIII by
Martha Popson
Published by The C. R. Gibson Company
Norwalk, Connecticut 06856
Printed in the United States of America
All rights reserved
ISBN 0-8378-2036-7

Remember:
You ARE NEVER ALONE!

Tonight I need to talk to You.

All the prayers I ever learned
don't quite say what I mean.

All that comes out is,
"Here I am, God — help!"

Those are all the words I know.
Still, it's some kind of prayer.

God,
some people seem
so secure
in their faith.
No matter what happens
they still believe.

I have so many questions:
Why do people suffer?
Why is life like this?
Are You really out there?
Is it okay to even ask these things?

I'm not me yet,
God.

I want to be
all that
I can be, but

I don't know
where to start.

Help me find
who I am.

Life is really
mixed up sometimes.

I can't make much
sense of it all

but, because of You,
I believe that
there are answers,
God,

even if I don't
know them just yet.

Faith is "I believe";
it's not "I know."

Maybe I couldn't prove in court
that You are good or that
You made me

but I do trust You,
God,
that these things
are true.

God,
some people think
they know all about You,
even how you look.

They say You are a man,
old and with a beard.

Others say we can call You
Mother, that You include
all things.

God, I'm having enough trouble
just deciding about my life.

God, I believe that
You are Truth and Beauty
and can wait for further details.

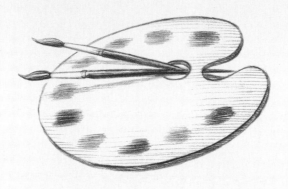

God, I was thinking
about all the colors
in the world:
reds and blues and yellows,
pinks and oranges and purples.

You could have made it
all in black and white,
and we never would have
known the difference.

Thanks, God, for the
technicolor touch.

Faith and feelings
aren't the same.

Sometimes I
forget that.

Help me, God,
to understand
that mad does not
equal bad,
that sad does not
equal sin,
that You still love me,
no matter how I feel just now,

that even when I
don't believe in
my goodness,
You do.

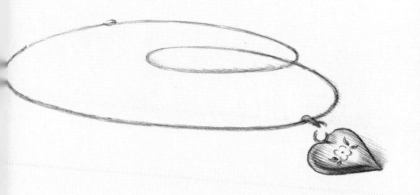

It's a good thing
that faith is a
gift.

It is sheer belief,
God, that You
love me right now.

People I love
got hurt today.

Why, God, why?

I'm waiting for
Your answer,
but all that
echoes is silence.

God, I'm trying
hard to believe
just now.

It is hard to hope
for the future, God.

I know people have felt
like this since the
beginning of time —

but so much seems wrong
in our world.
There is so little I
can do to change it.

I don't want to give up —
please, God,
show me some hope.

God,
You have seen
my many faces,
all of them,

the ones I show,
the ones I
carefully conceal.

You love them all.

I like to think
You laugh with me
when I clown.

God,
today I
feel good,
really good.

So many times
when I talk to You
I'm sad or worried
or confused.

Right now I like who I am,
the person You made me to be.

I just wanted You to know.

Two of my friends
had an argument, God.

It was over which
religion You like best.

Each one is sure that
their's is #1.

Maybe they need
to see that You
are The One.

There are times when
I think I'm a hopeless case,
that I'll never get my life
together, God.

I read that
"With faith
all things
are possible."

I guess that
includes
even me!

Not one thing
has gone right
since I got up
this morning.

Are you sure that
this is a day
that You have made?

God,
I really messed up today —
said all the wrong things,
hurt people's feelings,
couldn't make a move
without a mistake.

I didn't mean to do
any of it wrong,
but it still came out
that way.

I'm about to give up on me;
I hope it's true that You won't.

How can I feel so alone, God,
when I am surrounded by
so many people?

What is wrong with me, God?
Why can't I fit in?

God, help me not waste time
trying to be like someone else.

You've made me special,
an original.

You don't own a Xerox machine.

God,
the kids I hang out
with aren't bad,

but today
they decided to do
something we all
knew was wrong.

It was so hard
not to go along
with my friends.

Thanks for helping me
stand up for myself.

They say God has never
made a mistake

but I wonder if
You didn't goof
on me.

I'll have to trust
that You know
what You're doing

and, sooner or later,
I'll know, too.

I heard that Faith
is saying "yes"
to God.

I can't quite say "yes" yet, God,
but I sure don't mean "no."

Today I'm stuck in the
"maybe."

God, people
keep telling me
that these are the
best years of my life.

I sure hope they're wrong.

It doesn't feel so great
just now, and I don't know
how to fix it.

God, I feel selfish
for worrying about myself
when there are so many real
problems in the world.

But I need to understand
about me better before
the rest of it can
make much sense.

I don't understand, God.

They seem to know
all about You, and
some nights
I'm not even sure
if You are there.

God, I'm starting to see that
faith is not a straight line to You
where someone believes, one time,
and never wonders again.

Faith is a spiral that goes
around and around as we
grow towards You.

I'm not bad for doubting
sometimes, am I?

That's just the
way it goes.

Everytime I look at myself
I see someone different —
my whole life is changing,
my body, my moods, my dreams.

I'm so glad that all of this
is still part of Your plan for me.

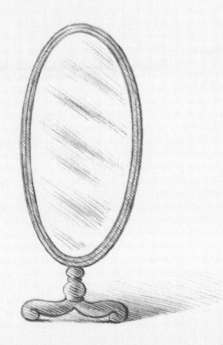

I'm changing so fast.

I've outgrown clothes
             friends
             old ideas

but one thing's for sure, God,
I can't outgrow You.

God, I sure don't know
why life goes on
as it does.

I do believe, though,
that You live
and You live in us.

When it comes right
down to it,
that is enough.

Faith is a gift,
God.

You made mine
unique.

No one else
will ever
have faith
quite like mine.

Thanks for picking it out
especially for me.

It is so quiet right now,
everyone else is sound asleep.

It's just You and I
here in the darkness.

I feel You in the Stillness.

God, I believe.

Interior illustrations by Nancy Hannans
Editorial direction by Jayne Bowman
Designed by Patrice Barrett
Set in Souvenir Light